CRAP TAXIDERMY

TO MY TIGER MOM, WENDY SU

SEE? I TOLD YOU I'D PUBLISH A BOOK ONE DAY.
WAIT, THIS ISN'T WHAT YOU HAD IN MIND?
DANGIT.

CRAP TAXIDERMY

KAT SU

TEN SPEED PRESS
BERKELEY

All rights reserved.
Published in the United States by Ten Speed Press, an imprint of the
Crown Publishing Group, a division of Random House LLC, a Penguin
Random House Company, New York.
www.crownpublishing.com
www.tenspeed.com

Ten Speed Press and the Ten Speed Press colophon are registered trademarks
of Random House LLC.

Originally published in Great Britain by Cassell, a division of Octopus
Publishing Group Ltd., an Hachette UK Company, London.

Library of Congress Cataloging-in-Publication Data is on file with the publisher.

Hardcover ISBN: 978-1-60774-820-5
eBook ISBN: 978-1-60774-821-2

Printed in China

Cover design by Margaux Keres

10 9 8 7 6 5 4 3 2 1

First American Edition

CONTENTS

INTRODUCTION

Taxidermy is a multidisciplinary artform. A competent taxidermist has an encyclopedic knowledge of anatomy, the laser-like precision of a world-class surgeon, and an artistic sensitivity to the physical world that rivals God Himself. The chances of a mere mortal mastering any of these traits is very slim, and the likelihood of becoming proficient in all three is virtually non-existent.

In the summer of 2009, I moved into an apartment in Brooklyn, New York, and aspired to give my sad living situation a touch of class by incorporating some dead animals into the decor. After scouring eBay and Etsy for taxidermy (a deer head to be precise), I quickly realized that the taxidermy available on the Internet could be classified into four categories:

1) Good taxidermy.
2) Bad taxidermy.
3) Weird-as-hell good taxidermy.
4) Weird-as-hell bad taxidermy.

Consequently, I launched the *Crappy Taxidermy* Tumblr to document the latter three categories. Since the site's creation, I have obsessively kept track of every bug-eyed, misshapen, bizarre, awkward, or just-plain-wrong piece of taxidermy that I was able to find online. As the site grew, readers started submitting photographs of their own taxidermy, and sightings of crappy taxidermy that they had found in museums, roadside attractions, stores, art galleries, or people's homes.

Considering all the weird, creepy taxidermy pictures I have accumulated on my hard drive since working on the *Crappy Taxidermy* blog, I had always speculated that I would be in jail by now for crimes against good taste.

However, I'm thrilled that the exact opposite has happened. This book is a celebration of crappy taxidermy and the eccentric and amazing people who create it. Regular taxidermy endeavors to give the illusion of life to the non-living, but crappy taxidermy highlights the subject's state of death due to the animal being contextualized in a completely surreal or absurd way. This book will present examples of taxidermy that is in a permanent state of rigor mortis, taxidermy that is so anatomically incorrect that it could be considered a crime against nature, and my personal favorite, taxidermy with hilarious over-the-top facial expressions.

The spirit of the book isn't meant to be disparaging, and I hope that people will delight in looking at the strange and preposterous specimens on display in these pages. A very special thank you to the taxidermists, fine artists, readers, and well-traveled photographers who contributed the pictures in this book.

IT'S IN THE EYES

10 **FOX WITH EYE TRANSPLANT**
SPOTTED IN CAIRO, EGYPT

BRUCE LEE

THE
WAY
OF THE
DRAGON
COLOUR

SIK
kido

PRODUCED BY
RAYMOND CHOW

WRITTEN and DIRECTED BY
BRUCE LEE

A GOLDEN HARVEST PR
RELEASED THROUGH CATH

KARATE-LOVING LIONESS
SPOTTED IN YORKSHIRE, UNITED KINGDOM

12 **BEST FRIENDS FOREVER**
SPOTTED IN NEW YORK, USA

EARNEST FOX
SPOTTED IN ST. PETERSBURG, RUSSIA

14 **FEARSOME BARN OWL**
SPOTTED IN OHIYA, SRI LANKA

FLAT WOLF
SPOTTED IN RHODES, GREECE

16 **EXTINCT BROWN BEAR**
SPOTTED IN NEWTOWN, AUSTRALIA

PREDATORY BROWN BEAR
SPOTTED IN STEYL, THE NETHERLANDS

18 **CRUSTY PANDA**
SPOTTED IN CHENGDU, CHINA

ALIEN-EYED SERVAL
SPOTTED IN KUCHING, MALAYSIA

20 **HUNGOVER CAT**
SPOTTED IN PYONGSONG, NORTH KOREA

EARLESS SNOW LEOPARD
SPOTTED IN POKHARA, NEPAL

HUNGRY HYPNOTIZED OCELOT
SPOTTED IN QUETZALTENANGO, GUATEMALA

ATTENTIVE SERVAL
SPOTTED IN STAVANGER, NORWAY

COCK-EYED BORNEAN CAT
SPOTTED IN KUCHING, MALAYSIA

DYNAMIC POSES

INCONGRUOUS RABBIT
SPOTTED IN JUBAIL, SAUDI ARABIA

SECRET LIFE OF OPOSSUMS
SPOTTED IN NAPIER, NEW ZEALAND

POUNCING ASIAN LEOPARD-CAT
SPOTTED IN KUCHING, MALAYSIA

30 **RIGID BOBCAT**
SPOTTED IN NORTH CAROLINA, USA

RIDING THE WOLF BUS
SPOTTED IN GANSU PROVINCE, CHINA

34 **FULLY ALERT BOBCAT**
SPOTTED IN NEW YORK, USA

GRIN & BEAR IT

على رجلين ومنهم من يمشي على أربع يخلق الله ما يشاء إن الله على

GROANING BOVINE
SPOTTED IN LONDON, UNITED KINGDOM

39

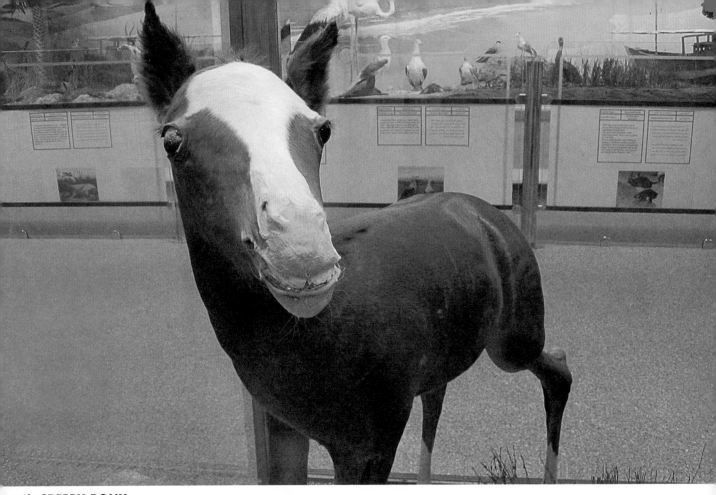

SPOTTED IN JUBAIL, SAUDI ARABIA

TABBY GYMNASTICS
SPOTTED IN MOSCOW, RUSSIA

41

FORTY-A-DAY LION
SPOTTED IN QALQILYA, STATE OF PALESTINE

LEERING HYENA
SPOTTED IN JUBAIL, SAUDI ARABIA

44 **TONSILS THE LYNX**
SPOTTED IN OREGON, USA

SNAGGLETOOTHED BAT
SPOTTED IN DUBLIN, REPUBLIC OF IRELAND

45

OVER-FRIENDLY DOG
SPOTTED IN GWANGJU, SOUTH KOREA

MOTH-EATEN WOLVES
SPOTTED IN KOCHKOR, KYRGYZSTAN

IMPROVING ON NATURE

VICTORIAN CEILING FAN
SPOTTED IN LONDON, UNITED KINGDOM

GUINEA PIG KNUCKLEDUSTER
SPOTTED IN BUDAPEST, HUNGARY

CYCLOPS MONSTER
SPOTTED IN JUBAIL, SAUDI ARABIA

WHERE DUCKS COME FROM
SPOTTED IN PARIS, FRANCE

21.10.14.3-10

54 **FURIOUS WOLPERTINGER**
SPOTTED IN NEW YORK, USA

CURIOUS WOLPERTINGER
SPOTTED IN ROTHENBURG, GERMANY

JACKRABBIT 2.0
SPOTTED IN TAURANGA, NEW ZEALAND

SIAMESE SHEEP
SPOTTED IN LONDON, UNITED KINGDOM

58 **RATIPEDE (SCIENTIFIC NAME *RATTUS BRACHIPODIA*)**
SPOTTED IN GEORGIA, USA

CREATIVE BEER BOTTLES
SPOTTED IN BREWDOG ADVERTISEMENT

59

STRANGE ANATOMY

GOOGLY-EYED PUFFER FISH
SPOTTED IN ULAN BATOR, MONGOLIA

63

64 **DIETING FOX**
SPOTTED IN BUDAPEST, HUNGARY

UNCOMFORTABLE COYOTE
SPOTTED IN LAKE TITICACA, PERU

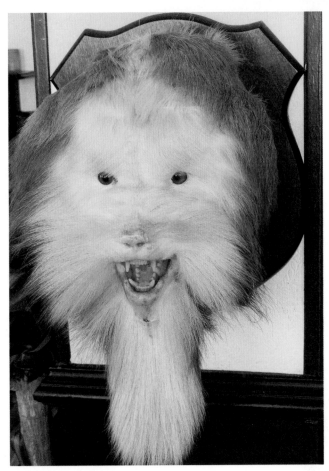

TASTEFUL "ASSQUATCH"
SPOTTED IN LONDON, UNITED KINGDOM

66 **FOX-CAT DUEL**
SPOTTED IN QALQILYA, STATE OF PALESTINE

ЭМПЕРОР ОЦОН ШУВУУ
Aptenodytes forsteri
Emperor penguin

CRESTFALLEN CAT

FIESTY JAGUAR

GANGLY RABBIT
SPOTTED IN HELSINKI, FINLAND

70 **SERENE COWS**
SPOTTED IN BUDAPEST, HUNGARY

ANTHROPOMORPHIC

IRATE MOLE
SPOTTED IN NEW YORK, USA

78 **MID-DEATH CRISIS**
SPOTTED IN YORKSHIRE, UNITED KINGDOM

BUSHBABY
SPOTTED IN TAURANGA, NEW ZEALAND

81

COWBOY OPOSSUM
SPOTTED IN GEORGIA, USA

RELAXED TOAD
SPOTTED IN SYDNEY, AUSTRALIA

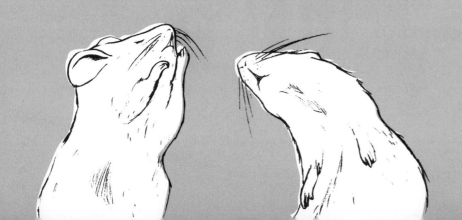

GET STUFFED

HOW TO STUFF YOUR OWN MOUSE

An interesting social consequence of working on a taxidermy blog is that everyone will start to ask you if you're a taxidermist. People are generally disappointed to find out that I'm actually a fashion designer, and that I was the kid who skipped Biology the day the class had to dissect a frog. Due to my squeamishness, I didn't think that I would ever see the day where I would have to do taxidermy but I needed to gain personal experience to execute this section of the book.

While I am by no means qualified to teach people how to stuff a mouse, an asset of working on a taxidermy blog is that I've met some bad-ass and talented individuals who are also taxidermists. One of these people is Daisy Tainton. I first met Daisy at a taxidermy contest in Brooklyn in 2009, and I was immediately drawn to her bright pink hair and dry sense of humor. Daisy was

on stage presenting dioramas of rhinoceros beetles in charming domestic settings (i.e., beetle sitting in a rocking chair knitting a sweater, beetle eating a plate of pasta alone), explaining that she was an Insect Preparator for the American Museum of Natural History, and that making beetle dioramas was one of her hobbies. When a judge facetiously asked her if her beetles ever got rowdy, she retorted: "No. They're quite sedate." In addition to being good with bugs, Daisy has stuffed various small- and medium-size mammals, birds, as well as various fantasy creatures courtesy of her healthy but

"SHOULD I ADD BOOBS TO HIM NOW? I SUPPOSE I CAN SORT THAT OUT LATER." —DAISY

perverse imagination. Another fun fact about Daisy is that she currently has a cat and a kitten in her freezer, despite being a vegetarian.

When I first approached Daisy to help me with this section of the book, I asked her to think of it as an "idiot-proof guide to mouse taxidermy" in hopes that even the most clumsy and squeamish person (such as myself) could do an adequate job on this project. There isn't much you can do about squeamishness, but the final result is a guide to mouse taxidermy utilizing materials that are cheap, forgiving, and easy to source. If you've ever been curious about taxidermy, I recommend grabbing a couple of funny, sarcastic friends and using this tutorial as basis for a bizarre weekend adventure.

TOTAL TIME: APPROXIMATELY 2 HOURS

READER BEWARE: WHATEVER YOU DO, DO NOT RUPTURE THE POOP SACK.

PREPARATION

Source your materials (see right). The most important one is your mouse, which can be procured from a pet store. I opted for frozen feeder mice (killed humanely by carbon dioxide gas) rather than a live one, for obvious reasons. The night before your taxidermy, remove the mouse from the freezer and allow to thaw in the refrigerator overnight. Be sure to liberate the mouse from its packaging if it is still wrapped. For storage, Daisy recommends using old plastic storage containers and resting the mouse on a bed of paper towels inside the container.

Daisy prefers working on a tray of loose borax as the borax will catch errant splashes of icky stuff that might occur during the process. Borax is a naturally occurring mineral compound that is available at most hardware stores or online. Borax substitutes are also available. Because borax has chemical properties that make it a desiccant, preservative, fungicide, and an insecticide, it has been commonly used in taxidermy as a moth-proofing and curing agent ever since toxic substances like arsenic were phased out of use.

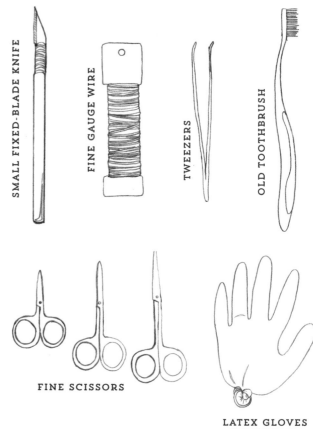

SMALL FIXED-BLADE KNIFE

FINE GAUGE WIRE

TWEEZERS

OLD TOOTHBRUSH

FINE SCISSORS

LATEX GLOVES
(OPTIONAL)

FROZEN MOUSE

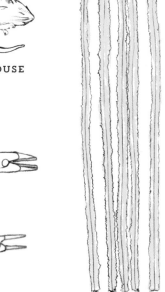

PIPE CLEANERS

CHILDREN'S
SELF-DRYING CLAY

BORAX

GOOGLY EYES OR
BALLPOINT PINS

AROMATHERAPY
CANDLE
(OPTIONAL)

WIRE CUTTERS

THREAD

SEWING
NEEDLES

CLEAR NAIL
POLISH

REMOVAL OF THE HIDE

1. Spread some borax on the work surface. Lay the mouse on its back and make a straight cut down its underbelly with your knife. Be aware of the mouse's internal organs and try not to puncture through the abdominal walls. Daisy states that while this doesn't ruin the hide, "the mess that it makes might ruin your day." Once the incision is made, stretch the skin away from the muscles and use your knife or a pair of scissors to help sever connective tissues (a).

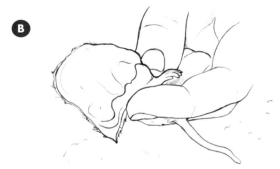

2. Your goal is to create a "mouse purse," where the hide is detached from the torso, but still attached at the limbs, head, and tail. Because the leg bones are tiny and mostly covered in cartilage, it is acceptable to leave them intact and attached to the hide. To achieve this, peel back the skin from the legs until you get to the ankle (b). Once you reach this point, take your wire cutters or scissors and snip at the ankle joint to liberate the legs from the rest of the body.

3. Next, separate the inside of the head from the inside of the rest of the body. Take your wire cutters and snip at the neck; if you're wondering what happens to the brains and the eyes after you do this, the answer is that you will have to scoop them out later.

c

4. At this point, the hide of your mouse should only be attached at the tail and the tail will need to be degloved. While this step is optional, Daisy highly recommends trying this step as it will allow you to manipulate the tail later. Otherwise, the tail will get withered and brittle as it dries. With degloving, the trick is to find a balance between firm and gentle, as the tail can tear very easily. Roll back the hide until you get a clear view of the base of the tail and use your fingers to push against the fold at the skin to extricate the skin from the bone structure (*c*). If you accidentally flip the tail inside out, use a pair of tweezers to rectify the situation.

5. To scoop out the brains, insert your knife into the skull cavity and remove the wet tissue. You probably won't be able to get everything, so make sure you pack a lot of borax into the head after you finish this step. Repeat the scooping part of this step with the eyes (*d*).

6. To cure the mouse hide, rub and clean the hide in the borax.

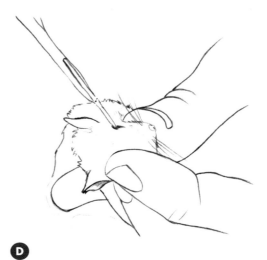

D

STUFFING THE MOUSE

7. Get your mouse properly wired. Cut off a piece of pipe cleaner and gently insert it through the tail. Next, cut off four pieces of fine-gauge wire and carefully string it through the mouse's limbs until it pierces through to the outside (e). There's no need to be exact here, as you can always snip excess later and the wire will allow you to manipulate the position of its arms and legs.

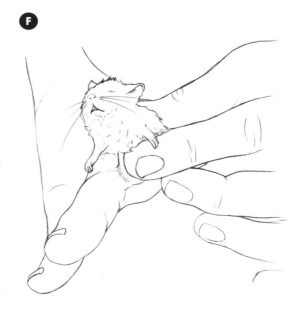

E

F

8. To stuff the mouse, begin by packing clay into the head to achieve the look of a fuller face, as Daisy explains, "because mice have so little fur on their faces, they can look a bit crumpled and crestfallen" (f).

G

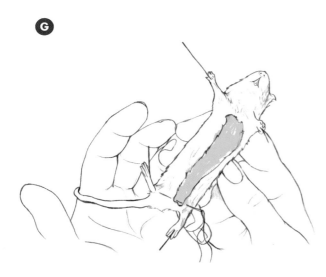

At this point, the clay and the wires will still be malleable. Position your mouse however you want; a sitting position is probably easiest, though (*h*).

H

9. Next, make a small pancake with the clay and then line the interior of the pelt. Use your judgement to determine the amount of clay that you should use, bearing in mind that there is typically 10 percent shrinkage after the clay fully dries. Stitch the incision closed with the needle and thread and keep the seam allowance small (*g*).

THE FINISHING TOUCHES

10. To set in the eyes, cut the ballpoint pins into ¼-inch/6mm nubs and pierce the pins through the eye sockets (*i*). You can also use another pin to manipulate the skin around the eye to create lids. Daisy also likes to run some nail polish over the eyeball to give the mouse an extra hint of life. If you're not using pins and want to make crappy taxidermy, use an adhesive to glue some googly eyes over the eye.

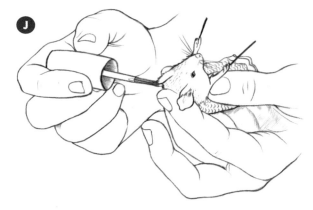

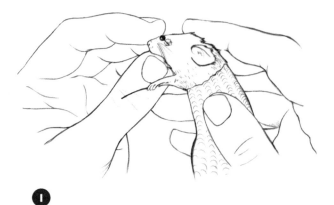

11. Next, take the clear nail polish and run it over the ears (*j*). This will give the ears more structure and stop them from folding in on themselves; it also instantly makes your mouse look perkier and more lifelike. Keep an eye on the ears as they dry because their natural proclivity is to collapse. Finally, take an old toothbrush and gently groom the mouse; toothbrush, borax, and some scrubbing will work out any blood stains still in the fur. Set your mouse to dry, and when it is dry, snip off the extra wire.

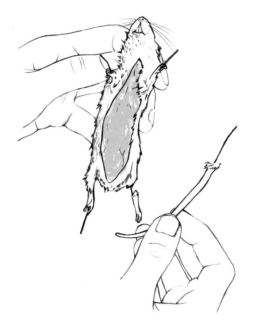

WHEN ACCIDENTS HAPPEN

Don't feel bad if accidents happen along the way. As an accident-prone person, I amputated two tails and one hind leg while I was stuffing my three mice. Daisy says that when this happens, you just have to improvise: "If you're making a diorama, and your mouse unexpectedly loses a leg, you'll know where you should probably put the miniature table." Since I wasn't working with any furniture props, I salvaged my amputated parts by stringing wire through them and reattaching the pieces to the main body with hot glue. Clearly, it's less than ideal, but it was still a workable solution for my purposes.

Mark Goldberg, Daisy Tainton, Meredith Zanotta, Daniel Mahem, David Melahz, Patricia Chang, Sarah Goldberg, Adam Cornish, Mark Goldblatt, Henry Welt, Allison Hunter, Tiffany Beveridge, Lisa Wolpert, Lawrence Swint, Yunusa Kenchi, Karin Reichert-Frei, Hannah Knowles, Pauline Bache, Tumblr & Octopus Books!

Finally, this book would not have been possible without these contributors:
Alexander Bunk (www.alexanderbunke.de), taxidermy by Cas Groooters (www.casperscreatures.com) 53; Alison Oddy (Flickr: WorldOfOddy) 11; Andrea (Flickr: hownowbrowncow2) 35; Andreas Vermulean 47; Andrew Lancaster, taxidermy by Andrew Lancaster 56, 81; Andrew Murray (Flickr: MrAndrewMurray) 10; Andy Deemer (www.asiaobscura.com) 63; Aodhnait Donnelly 79l; Becky (Flickr: Mandy_Moon), taxidermy by Becky 58; bighunter252 (eBay: bighunter252) 30; Bjørn Christian Tørrissen, (www.bjornfree.com) 14r, 20, 32, 45, 68l, 68r; Brad Traynor, freeze-dried by Brad Traynor 82r; BrewDog UK (www.brewdog.com) 59; Brian Glucroft (www.isidorsfugue.com) 18; Chris Fraser 46; Christian Novak 55; Daniel Tepper 31, 38, 42, 66; David Haberthür (Flickr: habi) 14l; Emily Binard (Etsy: ebinard), The Gowanus Mermouse 76r, Road Kill's Revenge 77; Emma Quail 33; Géza Szöll si (www.szollosi.eu), photography by Krisztián Zana (krisztianzana.com), Successful Hunting! 2007 28r, Boxer 2007 51l, Fox No.2 2010 64, Cows 2013 70; Hannah Knowles, taxidermy from The Viktor Wynd Museum of Curiosities 39, 50, 57; Hannah Knowles 65r; Ivie Morgan, taxidermy by Ivie Morgan 41; James Castleden (www.jamescastleden.com) 26, 40, 43, 51r; Jessie Hanz (Flickr: jessiebluejay) 71; Jon Chew (Flickr: Jonny_Chew) 19, 23, 29; Jon McClintock (Flickr: JonMcclintock) 21; Judit Aus 15; Julie Dermansky (www.jsdart.com) 28l; Karin 12, 17, 34, 54, 75; Kate Perris (Flickr: Dansette) 80; Kenneth Gjesdal (Flickr: Gjesdal) 22r; Marco Repola (Flickr: istolethetv) 67, 74; Megan (Flickr: TornadoGrrrl) 22l; Misha Davids (Flickr: Misha1138) 13; Paul Lim (Flickr: Fudj) 27, 76l; Sam Friedman (Flickr: Friedpixphoto) 79r; Sam Judson (Flickr: SamJudson) 65l; Sarah Burhouse, taxidermy by Sarah Burhouse (Etsy: snailsales) 78, 83; Sirja Ellen (Flickr: shaluna) 69; Thomas Monin (www.thomasmonin.com), Mafias I 2008, courtesy of Galerie Barnoud, Dijon, photograph by Phillippe Blanc 52; Tim Bradshaw 16; T.J. Edmond 82l; Yang Maoyuan, Horse No.3 2003,